Welcome to "Goal Setting for Personal and Professional Success"!
This written mini-course & workbook is designed to help you achieve your personal and professional goals by providing you with practical strategies for setting and achieving your objectives.

By completing this mini-course & the workbook exercises, you'll learn how to identify the goals that are most important to you, create a plan for achieving those goals, and stay motivated and focused along the way.

Whether you're just starting out in your career or looking to make positive changes in your personal life, this course is for you.

This whole process is self-paced, meaning you can complete it on your own schedule and at your own pace.

You'll have access to a range of resources, including worksheets, exercises, and additional reading materials, to help you apply the concepts and strategies covered in the course.

Throughout the course, you'll be encouraged to reflect on your progress, celebrate your successes, and identify areas for improvement. You'll also have the opportunity to connect with other learners in the course community and share your experiences and insights.

I'm thrilled that you've chosen to take this course, and I'm confident that the skills and strategies you'll learn here will help you achieve your personal and professional objectives.

At the end of the workbook are monthly, weekly & daily planning pages, that you can use to help keep you on track and consistently working achieve your goals.

So, let's get started!

HTTPS://KERRYWILLIAMS.UK

@iamkerrywilliams

Copyright | Kerry Williams | 2023 | Goal Setting for Personal and Professional Success

CONTENTS

Chapter 1: Understanding the Basics of Goal Setting
- ☐ 1.1 What are goals and why do we need them?
- ☐ 1.2 The importance of clarity and specificity when setting goals
- ☐ 1.3 Types of goals
- ☐ 1.4 SMART criteria for effective goal setting
- ☐ WS1.1 SMART goal-setting worksheet
- ☐ WS1.2 Goal clarity worksheet

Chapter 2: Setting Personal Goals
- ☐ 2.1 Identifying personal values and priorities
- ☐ 2.2 Setting personal goals that align with values and priorities
- ☐ 2.3 Overcoming common obstacles to achieving personal goals
- ☐ WS2.1 Values assessment worksheet
- ☐ WS2.2 Personal goal-setting worksheet

Chapter 3: Setting Professional Goals
- ☐ 3.1 Identifying career aspirations and professional development needs
- ☐ 3.2 Setting goals for career advancement, skill development, and job performance
- ☐ 3.3 Creating a plan to achieve professional goals
- ☐ WS3.1 Career development assessment worksheet
- ☐ WS3.2 Professional goal-setting worksheet

Chapter 4: Strategies for Goal Achievement
- ☐ 4.1 Creating a roadmap for achieving goals
- ☐ 4.2 Developing a plan for monitoring progress
- ☐ 4.3 Staying motivated and overcoming obstacles
- ☐ 4.4 Celebrating successes and learning from failures
- ☐ WS4.1 Action planning worksheet
- ☐ WS4.2 Progress monitoring worksheet

CHAPTER 1

CHAPTER 1: Understanding the Basics of Goal Setting

CHAPTER 1

Introduction

Setting goals is an important part of personal and professional success, but it's not always easy to do. To be effective, goals need to be specific, measurable, achievable, relevant, and time-bound. These criteria are often referred to as the SMART framework, and they provide a roadmap for setting goals that are clear, focused, and achievable.

Here's a breakdown of each element of the SMART framework:

1. Specific: Your goals should be specific and well-defined. This means they should answer the questions: What do I want to achieve? Why is it important to me? Who is involved? What resources do I need?
2. Measurable: Your goals should be measurable, so you can track your progress and see how far you've come. This means you should include a specific metric or target that you can use to measure your progress.
3. Achievable: Your goals should be challenging but achievable. This means they should stretch you outside of your comfort zone, but still be realistic and within your reach. When setting goals, consider your skills, resources, and time constraints.
4. Relevant: Your goals should be relevant to your values and priorities. This means they should align with your long-term aspirations and be meaningful to you. When setting goals, consider what you truly want to achieve and why it's important to you.
5. Time-bound: Your goals should have a specific deadline or timeline. This means you should include a specific date or timeframe by which you want to achieve your goal.

CHAPTER 1

By following these SMART criteria, you can set goals that are clear, focused, and achievable. In addition to the SMART criteria, it's also important to make sure your goals are written down and visible, so you can stay focused and motivated. You can use tools like a planner, calendar, or vision board to help keep your goals front and centre.

Setting effective goals is a key skill for personal and professional success, and the SMART framework provides a useful tool for making sure your goals are well-defined and achievable.

In the next module, we'll dive deeper into how to set personal goals that align with your values and priorities.

CHAPTER 1.1

Chapter 1.1
What are goals and why do we need them?

> **Goals are the targets we set for ourselves that help us achieve our personal and professional aspirations. They provide a sense of direction and purpose, help us stay motivated and focused, and allow us to measure our progress over time. Without goals, it's easy to feel lost or directionless, without a clear idea of what we want to achieve or how to get there.**

Goals can take many forms, from short-term objectives to long-term aspirations. Some common types of goals include:

- Personal goals: Goals related to personal growth and development, such as learning a new skill, traveling to a new place, or improving your physical health.
- Professional goals: Goals related to career advancement and development, such as getting a promotion, improving your job performance, or starting your own business.
- Educational goals: Goals related to academic achievement, such as earning a degree or learning a new language.
- Relationship goals: Goals related to improving your relationships with others, such as improving communication skills or spending more quality time with loved ones.

Regardless of the type of goal, setting goals is important because it gives us something to strive for and helps us grow and develop as individuals. Goals provide a sense of direction and purpose, and can help us overcome obstacles and challenges along the way.
In addition to providing direction and motivation, setting goals can also help us achieve a sense of fulfilment and accomplishment. When we set goals and work hard to achieve them, we experience a sense of satisfaction and pride that can be incredibly rewarding.
Overall, goals are an essential part of personal and professional success. By setting clear, focused goals and developing a plan to achieve them, we can take control of our lives and achieve things we might not have thought possible

CHAPTER 1.2

Chapter 1.2
The importance of clarity and specificity when setting goals

> When setting goals, it's important to be clear and specific about what you want to achieve. Vague or ambiguous goals can be hard to measure and difficult to achieve, which can make it hard to stay motivated and focused. By contrast, clear and specific goals give you a clear target to aim for, making it easier to stay on track and measure your progress.

Here are some reasons why clarity and specificity are important when setting goals:

1. Helps you identify your priorities: When you're clear and specific about your goals, it becomes easier to identify what's most important to you. This can help you prioritize your time and resources, making it easier to achieve your goals.

2. Makes it easier to measure progress: When your goals are specific, you can easily track your progress and measure how far you've come. This can be incredibly motivating and help you stay focused on your goals.

3. Helps you stay motivated: When your goals are clear and specific, you have a clear target to aim for. This can be incredibly motivating, giving you a sense of purpose and direction as you work towards your goals.

4. Makes it easier to identify obstacles: When your goals are specific, it becomes easier to identify potential obstacles and develop a plan to overcome them. This can help you stay focused and stay on track, even when faced with challenges or setbacks.

To make your goals clear and specific, it's important to be as detailed as possible when setting them. Use the SMART framework to help you set goals that are Specific, Measurable, Achievable, Relevant, and Time-bound. This means setting goals that are well-defined, have clear metrics for success, are realistic and achievable, are relevant to your values and priorities, and have a specific deadline or timeline.

CHAPTER 1.3

Chapter 1.3
Types of goals: short-term vs. long-term, personal vs. professional, etc.

Goals come in many shapes and sizes, and can be classified in a variety of ways. Here are some common ways to categorise goals:

1. Short-term vs. long-term goals: Short-term goals are goals that you can achieve in the near future, typically within a few months or a year. Long-term goals are goals that you hope to achieve over a longer period of time, typically several years or more. Short-term goals are often stepping stones towards achieving long-term goals.
2. Personal vs. professional goals: Personal goals are goals that relate to your personal growth and development, such as improving your health or learning a new skill. Professional goals are goals that relate to your career, such as getting a promotion or starting your own business. While personal and professional goals can be closely linked, it's important to set goals in both areas to achieve a well-rounded sense of fulfillment and success.
3. Process vs. outcome goals: Process goals are goals that relate to the actions or behaviours you need to take to achieve a desired outcome. For example, a process goal might be to exercise for 30 minutes every day, with the outcome goal of losing weight or improving your physical fitness. Outcome goals are goals that relate to the end result you want to achieve. For example, an outcome goal might be to run a marathon or publish a book.
4. Achievement vs. development goals: Achievement goals are goals that relate to accomplishing something specific, such as getting a degree or winning a competition. Development goals are goals that relate to improving a skill or area of knowledge, such as learning a new language or developing your leadership skills. Both types of goals are important for personal and professional growth.

CHAPTER 1.3

5. Tangible vs. intangible goals: Tangible goals are goals that can be measured or observed, such as earning a certain amount of money or completing a project. Intangible goals are goals that relate to qualities or values, such as improving your confidence or becoming more compassionate.

Ultimately, the type of goals you set will depend on your personal values, priorities, and aspirations. By setting a mix of short-term and long-term, personal and professional, process and outcome, achievement and development, and tangible and intangible goals, you can create a well-rounded approach to achieving your personal and professional aspirations.

CHAPTER 1.4

Chapter 1.4
SMART criteria for effective goal setting

The SMART framework is a useful tool for setting effective goals. The framework consists of five criteria that help ensure your goals are Specific, Measurable, Achievable, Relevant, and Time-bound.

Here's a breakdown of each element of the SMART framework:

1. Specific: Your goals should be specific and well-defined. This means they should answer the questions: What do I want to achieve? Why is it important to me? Who is involved? What resources do I need?

Example of a specific goal: "I want to lose 10 pounds in the next three months by exercising for 30 minutes every day and eating a balanced diet."

2. Measurable: Your goals should be measurable, so you can track your progress and see how far you've come. This means you should include a specific metric or target that you can use to measure your progress.

Example of a measurable goal: "I want to increase my sales by 20% by the end of the year."

3. Achievable: Your goals should be challenging but achievable. This means they should stretch you outside of your comfort zone, but still be realistic and within your reach. When setting goals, consider your skills, resources, and time constraints.

Example of an achievable goal: "I want to complete a 5k race in three months, even though I've never run more than a mile before. I'll start by running for 10 minutes a day and gradually increasing my distance."

CHAPTER 1.4

4. Relevant: Your goals should be relevant to your values and priorities. This means they should align with your long-term aspirations and be meaningful to you. When setting goals, consider what you truly want to achieve and why it's important to you.

Example of a relevant goal: "I want to start my own business in the next two years, because I value independence and creativity and want to be my own boss."

5. Time-bound: Your goals should have a specific deadline or timeline. This means you should include a specific date or time frame by which you want to achieve your goal.

Example of a time-bound goal: "I want to finish writing my novel by the end of the year, by committing to writing for one hour every day and attending a writing workshop."

By following these SMART criteria, you can set goals that are clear, focused, and achievable.

In the next module, we'll explore how to apply the SMART framework to different types of goals, and show you how to create an action plan for achieving your goals.

WORKSHEET 1.1

Self-assessment worksheet

Instructions: Reflect on your current goal-setting practices and answer the questions below. Be honest with yourself and try to identify areas where you can improve your goal-setting skills.

1. How often do you set goals for yourself? (daily, weekly, monthly, quarterly, annually, never)

2. How do you usually set goals? (write them down, discuss them with others, keep them in your head, etc.)

3. Do you use the SMART criteria when setting goals? (yes, sometimes, no)

4. How specific are your goals? (clearly defined, vague, general)

5. How measurable are your goals? (have specific metrics or targets, unclear how to measure progress)

6. How achievable are your goals? (realistic, unrealistic, too easy)

WORKSHEET 1.1

7. How relevant are your goals to your personal or professional aspirations? (aligned, not aligned)

8. How time-bound are your goals? (have specific deadlines or timelines, open-ended)

9. How do you track your progress towards your goals? (use metrics or targets, keep track in your head, don't track progress)

How do you stay motivated and overcome obstacles when working towards your goals? (seek support from others, stay focused on your why, visualize success, celebrate small wins, etc.)

Now that you have completed the self-assessment, reflect on your answers and identify areas where you can improve your goal-setting skills. Consider setting more specific and measurable goals, using the SMART criteria, tracking your progress towards your goals, and staying motivated by celebrating small wins and seeking support from others. By using these strategies, you can improve your goal-setting skills and achieve success in all areas of your life.

WORKSHEET 1.2

Goal-Setting Reflection Worksheet

Instructions: Use the questions below to reflect on why you want to set goals and what you hope to achieve through the "Goal Setting for Personal and Professional Success" course

1. What are your personal and professional aspirations? (e.g., career advancement, improved health and wellness, financial stability, etc.)

2. Why are these goals important to you? (e.g., to provide for your family, to achieve personal fulfillment, to make a positive impact on the world, etc.)

3. What are some obstacles that have prevented you from achieving your goals in the past? (e.g., lack of motivation, lack of time or resources, fear of failure, etc.)

WORKSHEET 1.2

4. How do you hope to benefit from setting and achieving your goals? (e.g., improved self-confidence, greater sense of purpose, enhanced job satisfaction, etc.)

5. What specific skills or strategies do you hope to learn from the course? (e.g., how to set SMART goals, how to stay motivated, how to overcome obstacles, etc.)

6. How will you apply what you learn in the course to your personal and professional life? (e.g., by setting specific and measurable goals, by tracking progress and celebrating successes, by seeking support from others, etc.)

Now that you have completed the reflection worksheet, use your answers to set specific and achievable goals for yourself, and use the skills and strategies you learn in the course to achieve those goals. Remember to stay focused on your why, celebrate small wins, and seek support from others along the way. Good luck!

CHAPTER 2

CHAPTER 2:
Setting Personal Goals

CHAPTER 2

Introduction

Setting personal goals is an important part of personal growth and development. Personal goals can help you improve your physical and mental health, learn new skills, pursue hobbies and interests, and develop deeper relationships with others. When setting personal goals, it's important to consider what's truly important to you and what you want to achieve.

Here are some steps you can follow to set personal goals:

1. Identify your values: Your personal goals should align with your values and priorities. Take some time to reflect on what's most important to you, and use this as a starting point for setting personal goals.
2. Brainstorm ideas: Make a list of personal goals you'd like to achieve. This can include things like learning a new language, taking up a new hobby, improving your physical health, or deepening your relationships with loved ones.
3. Prioritise your goals: Once you have a list of personal goals, prioritize them based on what's most important to you. This will help you focus your time and resources on the goals that matter most.
4. Make your goals SMART: Use the SMART framework to make your personal goals specific, measurable, achievable, relevant, and time-bound.
5. Create an action plan: Once you have a list of SMART personal goals, create an action plan to achieve them. This can include breaking down larger goals into smaller, more manageable steps, setting deadlines and milestones, and identifying potential obstacles and ways to overcome them.

CHAPTER 2

Example of a personal goal:

Goal: "I want to improve my physical fitness by running a 5k race in six months."

SMART CRITERIA:

- Specific: I want to run a 5k race in six months.
- Measurable: I will track my progress by running three times a week and gradually increasing my distance.
- Achievable: I will start by running for 10 minutes a day and gradually increasing my distance.
- Relevant: I value physical health and want to challenge myself to achieve a new goal.
- Time-bound: I will run the 5k race in six months.

ACTION PLAN:

- Week 1-2: Run for 10 minutes a day, three times a week.
- Week 3-4: Increase running time to 15 minutes a day, three times a week.
- Week 5-6: Increase running time to 20 minutes a day, three times a week.
- Week 7-8: Increase running time to 25 minutes a day, three times a week.
- Week 9-10: Increase running time to 30 minutes a day, three times a week.
- Week 11-12: Increase running time to 35 minutes a day, three times a week.
- Week 13-14: Increase running time to 40 minutes a day, three times a week.
- Week 15-16: Increase running time to 45 minutes a day, three times a week.
- Week 17-18: Run for 30 minutes a day, five times a week.
- Week 19-20: Run for 45 minutes a day, five times a week.
- Week 21-22: Run for 60 minutes a day, five times a week.
- Week 23-24: Run for 75 minutes a day, five times a week.
- Week 25-26: Run for 90 minutes a day, five times a week.

By setting personal goals that are important to you and developing an action plan to achieve them, you can take control of your personal growth and development and achieve things you might not have thought possible.

Chapter 2.1
Identifying personal values and priorities

Identifying your personal values and priorities is an important step in setting meaningful and fulfilling goals. Your personal values are the things that matter most to you, while your priorities are the things that require your attention and focus. When you understand your values and priorities, you can make decisions and set goals that align with what's truly important to you.

Here are some steps you can follow to identify your personal values and priorities:

1. Reflect on what matters to you: Take some time to reflect on the things that matter most to you. This can include your relationships with loved ones, your personal beliefs and values, your passions and interests, and your personal goals and aspirations.
2. Create a list of values: Based on your reflection, create a list of values that represent what's most important to you. These might include things like honesty, integrity, compassion, and personal growth.
3. Prioritise your values: Once you have a list of values, prioritise them based on what's most important to you. This can help you understand which values are central to your sense of identity and well-being.
4. Identify your priorities: Your priorities are the things that require your attention and focus, such as your family, your career, your health, or your personal development. Take some time to identify your priorities and rank them in order of importance.
5. Align your goals with your values and priorities: Once you have a clear understanding of your values and priorities, use this information to set goals that align with what's truly important to you. This can help you stay motivated and focused, and increase your chances of achieving your goals.

CHAPTER 2.1

Example of identifying personal values and priorities:

Values:
- Integrity
- Compassion
- Personal growth
- Creativity
- Authenticity

Priorities:
1. Family
2. Career
3. Health
4. Personal development

By identifying your personal values and priorities, you can set goals that align with what's most important to you. For example, if you value personal growth and prioritise your career, you might set a goal to learn a new skill or pursue a professional certification. Or, if you value authenticity and prioritise your health, you might set a goal to try a new form of exercise or explore a new hobby that aligns with your values. By aligning your goals with your values and priorities, you can create a sense of purpose and meaning in your life, and achieve personal and professional success on your own terms.

CHAPTER 2.2

Chapter 2.2
Setting personal goals that align with values and priorities

> **Setting personal goals that align with your values and priorities is essential for creating a fulfilling and meaningful life. When your goals align with what's truly important to you, you're more likely to stay motivated, focused, and committed to achieving them. Here are some steps you can follow to set personal goals that align with your values and priorities:**

1. Review your values and priorities: Take some time to review your personal values and priorities. This can help you understand what's truly important to you and what you want to achieve.
2. Brainstorm ideas: Based on your values and priorities, brainstorm a list of personal goals you'd like to achieve. This can include things like learning a new skill, pursuing a hobby or interest, improving your health, or deepening your relationships with loved ones.
3. Prioritise your goals: Once you have a list of personal goals, prioritise them based on how well they align with your values and priorities. This can help you focus your time and resources on the goals that matter most.
4. Make your goals SMART: Use the SMART framework to make your personal goals specific, measurable, achievable, relevant, and time-bound.
5. Create an action plan: Once you have a list of SMART personal goals, create an action plan to achieve them. This can include breaking down larger goals into smaller, more manageable steps, setting deadlines and milestones, and identifying potential obstacles and ways to overcome them.

CHAPTER 2.2

Example of setting personal goals that align with values and priorities:

Values:
- Creativity
- Health
- Personal growth

Priorities:
1. Family
2. Career
3. Travel

Personal Goals:
1. Learn to play the guitar by taking weekly lessons for six months, to fulfill the value of creativity.
2. Complete a 5K race in three months, to fulfill the value of health.
3. Attend a personal development seminar or workshop within six months, to fulfill the value of personal growth.

SMART criteria:
- Specific: Learn to play the guitar by taking weekly lessons for six months, complete a 5K race in three months, attend a personal development seminar or workshop within six months.
- Measurable: Track progress by taking weekly lessons, tracking exercise routine, and attending the seminar/workshop.
- Achievable: Set a realistic timeline and allocate resources (time, budget, equipment, etc.) accordingly.
- Relevant: Align the goals with personal values and priorities.
- Time-bound: Set deadlines or milestones for each goal.

CHAPTER 2.2

Action plan:

- Week 1-4: Attend guitar lessons once a week, practice for 30 minutes every day.
- Week 5-8: Attend guitar lessons once a week, practice for 45 minutes every day.
- Week 9-12: Attend guitar lessons once a week, practice for 60 minutes every day.
- Week 13: Participate in the 5K race.
- Week 14-16: Attend a personal development seminar or workshop.

By setting personal goals that align with your values and priorities, you can create a sense of purpose and meaning in your life, and achieve personal and professional success on your own terms. Remember to revisit and revise your goals regularly, as your values and priorities may change over time.

CHAPTER 2.3

Chapter 2.3
Overcoming common obstacles to achieving personal goals

Achieving personal goals can be challenging, and it's not uncommon to encounter obstacles along the way. Here are some common obstacles to achieving personal goals and some strategies for overcoming them:

1. Lack of motivation: One of the most common obstacles to achieving personal goals is a lack of motivation. When you don't feel motivated, it's easy to procrastinate or give up on your goals altogether.

Solution: Find ways to stay motivated by reminding yourself of your values, visualising your success, and celebrating small wins along the way. You can also enlist the support of friends or family members who can help keep you accountable and motivated.

2. Time constraints: Another common obstacle to achieving personal goals is a lack of time. It's easy to get bogged down with work, family obligations, and other responsibilities, leaving little time for personal pursuits.

Solution: Prioritise your goals and schedule time for them on your calendar. Identify small pockets of time throughout the day when you can work on your goals, such as during your commute or during your lunch break.

3. Lack of resources: Some personal goals may require resources you don't currently have, such as money, equipment, or support from others.

Solution: Identify the resources you need to achieve your goals and explore ways to obtain them. This might include taking on a part-time job to save money, borrowing equipment from a friend, or seeking support from a mentor or coach.

CHAPTER 2.3

4. Fear of failure: Fear of failure can be a major obstacle to achieving personal goals. When you're afraid of failing, it's easy to give up before you even start.

Solution: Embrace the possibility of failure and reframe it as an opportunity for growth and learning. Remember that setbacks are a natural part of the process and that each failure brings you one step closer to success.

5. Lack of support: Finally, a lack of support from friends, family, or colleagues can be an obstacle to achieving personal goals. When you don't feel supported, it can be challenging to stay motivated and committed to your goals.

Solution: Surround yourself with supportive people who believe in you and your goals. Seek out a mentor or coach who can provide guidance and accountability. Join a community or group that shares your interests and goals.

By recognizing and overcoming common obstacles to achieving personal goals, you can stay on track and achieve the success you desire. Remember to stay flexible and open to adjusting your goals and strategies as needed, and to celebrate your progress along the way.

WORKSHEET 2.1

SMART Goal-Setting Worksheet

Instructions: Use the questions below to guide you through the process of setting SMART goals for yourself

SPECIFIC:

What specific goal do you want to achieve? (e.g., "I want to lose 10 pounds in the next 3 months.")

MEASURABLE:

How will you measure progress towards your goal? (e.g., "I will track my weight and waist circumference weekly and aim to lose 1-2 pounds per week.")

ACHIEVABLE:

Is the goal achievable and realistic for you? (e.g., "Based on my current diet and exercise habits, I believe I can realistically lose 10 pounds in 3 months.")

WORKSHEET 2.1

RELEVANT:
Is the goal relevant to your personal or professional aspirations? (e.g., "Losing weight will improve my health and well-being, and help me feel more confident in my personal and professional life.")

TIME-BOUND:
What is the deadline for achieving your goal? (e.g., "I will achieve my goal of losing 10 pounds by June 30th, which is 3 months from now.")

Now that you have set a SMART goal, create an action plan for achieving it. Identify the specific steps you will take to achieve your goal, and the resources and support you will need along the way. Remember to track your progress, celebrate small wins, and adjust your plan as needed to stay on track towards your goal. Good luck!

WORKSHEET 2.2

Goal Clarity Worksheet

> Instructions: Use the questions below to clarify what you want to achieve and why it's important to you.

1. What is your goal? (e.g., "I want to start my own business.")

2. Why is this goal important to you? (e.g., "I want to have more control over my career and financial future.")

3. What are the benefits of achieving this goal? (e.g., "I will have more flexibility in my work schedule, the potential to earn more income, and the satisfaction of creating something of my own.")

WORKSHEET 2.2

4. Who will benefit from you achieving this goal? (e.g., "My family will benefit from the added income, and my customers will benefit from the product or service I provide.")

5. What are the potential obstacles to achieving this goal? (e.g., "Lack of funding, lack of business experience, or competition in the market.")

6. What specific steps can you take to overcome these obstacles? (e.g., "I can research funding options, seek advice from experienced entrepreneurs, or differentiate my product or service from competitors.")

WORKSHEET 2.2

7. What support or resources do you need to achieve this goal? (e.g., "I may need financial support, mentoring, or a network of contacts in my industry.")

Now that you have clarified your goal and why it's important to you, create an action plan for achieving it. Identify the specific steps you will take to achieve your goal, and the resources and support you will need along the way. Remember to track your progress, celebrate small wins, and adjust your plan as needed to stay on track towards your goal.

CHAPTER 3:
Setting Professional Goals

CHAPTER 3

Introduction

Setting professional goals is an important part of career development and growth. Professional goals can help you improve your skills, advance your career, and achieve greater job satisfaction. When setting professional goals, it's important to consider your current job or career path and where you want to go.

Set Goals

Here are some steps you can follow to set professional goals:

1. Assess your current situation: Take stock of your current job or career path, including your strengths, weaknesses, and areas for improvement. Consider where you want to be in the next 1-3 years, and what steps you need to take to get there.
2. Identify areas for improvement: Based on your assessment, identify areas where you could improve your skills or knowledge. This might include taking on new responsibilities, pursuing professional development opportunities, or seeking out a mentor or coach.
3. Set specific goals: Use the SMART framework to set specific, measurable, achievable, relevant, and time-bound goals. These might include goals related to skill development, job performance, or career advancement.
4. Develop an action plan: Once you have a list of SMART professional goals, develop an action plan to achieve them. This might include identifying resources you need, breaking down larger goals into smaller steps, and setting deadlines and milestones.

CHAPTER 3

Example of a professional goal:

Goal: "I want to improve my leadership skills by attending a leadership development program within the next six months."

SMART criteria:

- Specific: Attend a leadership development program within the next six months.
- Measurable: Complete the program and receive a certificate of completion.
- Achievable: Research and select a reputable program, and obtain necessary approvals and funding from my employer.
- Relevant: Enhance my leadership skills and advance my career.
- Time-bound: Complete the program within the next six months.

Action plan:

- Week 1-2: Research and identify potential leadership development programs.
- Week 3-4: Obtain approvals and funding from my employer.
- Week 5-6: Register for the program and begin attending sessions.
- Week 7-8: Complete required coursework and assignments.
- Week 9-10: Attend additional sessions and networking events.
- Week 11-12: Complete the program and receive a certificate of completion.

By setting professional goals that align with your career path and aspirations, you can advance your skills and knowledge, increase your job satisfaction, and achieve greater success in your career. Remember to revisit and revise your goals regularly, and to seek out feedback and support from colleagues and mentors along the way.

CHAPTER 3.1

Chapter 3.1
Identifying career aspirations and professional development needs

Identifying your career aspirations and professional development needs is an important step in setting professional goals and advancing your career. Career aspirations are your long-term career goals, while professional development needs are the skills or knowledge you need to develop to achieve those goals.

Here are some steps you can follow to identify your career aspirations and professional development needs:

1. Reflect on your current situation: Take some time to reflect on your current job or career path, and where you want to be in the future. Consider your interests, values, and skills, and think about what kind of work would be fulfilling and meaningful to you.
2. Research career paths: Research different career paths that align with your interests and values. Consider the education or experience required for those careers, and whether you have the necessary skills or knowledge.
3. Identify your strengths and weaknesses: Identify your strengths and weaknesses, and consider the skills or knowledge you need to develop to achieve your career aspirations.
4. Set career goals: Based on your reflection and research, set long-term career goals that align with your values and aspirations.
5. Develop a professional development plan: Develop a professional development plan that outlines the skills or knowledge you need to develop to achieve your career goals. This might include taking courses, attending workshops or conferences, seeking out a mentor or coach, or pursuing additional education or certification.

CHAPTER 3.1

Example of identifying career aspirations and professional development needs:

Career aspirations:
- To become a senior project manager in my current industry within the next five years.
- To transition to a new industry in a leadership role within the next seven years.

Professional development needs:
- Advanced project management skills and knowledge, including risk management and budgeting.
- Industry-specific knowledge and expertise in the new industry, such as regulations and trends.

Professional development plan:
- Take a project management course focused on risk management within the next six months.
- Attend a budgeting workshop within the next three months.
- Seek out a mentor who has experience in the new industry, and schedule regular meetings to discuss industry-specific knowledge and trends.
- Research and enrol in a certificate program or degree program in the new industry within the next two years.

By identifying your career aspirations and professional development needs, you can set meaningful and fulfilling career goals and develop the skills and knowledge you need to achieve them. Remember to revisit and revise your goals and professional development plan regularly, and to seek out feedback and support from colleagues and mentors along the way.

CHAPTER 3.2

Chapter 3.2
Setting goals for career advancement, skill development, and job performance

Setting goals for career advancement, skill development, and job performance is essential for professional growth and success. Here are some steps you can follow to set goals in these areas:

1. Career Advancement Goals: Identify the career advancement goals that align with your long-term career aspirations. This might include goals related to job title, salary, or responsibility.

Example: "I want to become a team leader within my department within the next two years."

2. Skill Development Goals: Identify the skills or knowledge you need to develop to achieve your career goals. This might include skills related to your current job or skills that are necessary for the job you want.

Example: "I need to develop my leadership skills, including delegation, conflict resolution, and communication."

3. Job Performance Goals: Identify the job performance goals that will help you excel in your current role and prepare you for future opportunities. This might include goals related to productivity, efficiency, or quality of work.

Example: "I want to increase my productivity by 10% in the next quarter by developing a more efficient workflow and using productivity tools."

CHAPTER 3.2

4. Set SMART Goals: Use the SMART framework to set specific, measurable, achievable, relevant, and time-bound goals in each area.

Example of setting SMART goals:
Career Advancement Goal:
- Specific: Become a team leader within my department within the next two years.
- Measurable: Achieve a promotion to a team leader position.
- Achievable: Develop the necessary leadership skills and knowledge, and demonstrate strong performance in my current role.
- Relevant: Aligns with my long-term career aspirations.
- Time-bound: Achieve the promotion within the next two years.

Skill Development Goal:
- Specific: Develop my leadership skills, including delegation, conflict resolution, and communication, within the next six months.
- Measurable: Complete a leadership development course and apply the skills in my current role.
- Achievable: Research and select a reputable leadership development course, obtain necessary approvals and funding from my employer.
- Relevant: Aligns with my career advancement goal.
- Time-bound: Complete the course and apply the skills within the next six months.

Job Performance Goal:
- Specific: Increase my productivity by 10% in the next quarter by developing a more efficient workflow and using productivity tools.
- Measurable: Track progress using productivity tools and measure productivity gains.
- Achievable: Develop a more efficient workflow and explore productivity tools that fit my work style and needs.
- Relevant: Improves my job performance and prepares me for future opportunities.
- Time-bound: Achieve the 10% productivity gain within the next quarter

CHAPTER 3.2

By setting goals for career advancement, skill development, and job performance, you can develop the skills and knowledge you need to succeed in your career and achieve your long-term aspirations. Remember to revisit and revise your goals regularly, and to seek out feedback and support from colleagues and mentors along the way.

CHAPTER 3.3

Chapter 3.3
Creating a plan to achieve professional goals

Creating a plan to achieve professional goals is an essential step in turning your aspirations into reality. Here are some steps you can follow to create a plan to achieve your professional goals:

1. Break down your goals: Break down your professional goals into smaller, more manageable tasks or milestones. This will help you track your progress and stay motivated.
2. Prioritise your tasks: Prioritise your tasks based on their importance and urgency. Identify the tasks that require immediate action and those that can be addressed at a later time.
3. Create a timeline: Create a timeline that outlines when you will complete each task or milestone. This will help you stay on track and meet your deadlines.
4. Identify resources: Identify the resources you need to achieve your goals, such as financial resources, equipment, or support from others.
5. Develop a support system: Develop a support system that can help you stay accountable and motivated. This might include friends, family, colleagues, or a mentor or coach.

Example of a plan to achieve a professional goal:

Goal: "I want to become a certified project manager within the next year."

Tasks:

- Research project management certification programs.
- Select a program that meets my needs and goals.
- Obtain funding and approval from my employer.
- Complete the required coursework and assignments.
- Prepare for and pass the certification exam.
- Receive certification.

Timeline:
- Month 1-2: Research project management certification programs.
- Month 3-4: Select a program that meets my needs and goals.
- Month 5-6: Obtain funding and approval from my employer.
- Month 7-10: Complete the required coursework and assignments.
- Month 11: Prepare for and take the certification exam.
- Month 12: Receive certification.

Resources:
- Project management certification program
- Funding and approval from my employer
- Study materials and resources for the certification exam

Support System:
- A mentor or coach who can provide guidance and support
- A study group or community of other project managers pursuing certification

By creating a plan to achieve your professional goals, you can break down your aspirations into smaller, more manageable tasks, and stay on track to achieving your long-term career aspirations. Remember to stay flexible and open to adjusting your plan as needed, and to seek out feedback and support from colleagues and mentors along the way.

WORKSHEET 3.1

Values Assessment Worksheet

Instructions: Use the questions below to assess your personal values and how they relate to your goals.

1. What are your top 5 personal values? (e.g., family, health, integrity, creativity, growth)
   1.
   2.
   3.
   4.
   5.

2. Why are these values important to you? (e.g., "Family is important to me because they provide love and support, and give me a sense of belonging.")

   1.

   2.

   3.

   4.

   5.

WORKSHEET 3.1

3. How do your values influence your goals? (e.g., "My value of creativity influences my goal to start a side business selling my artwork.")

4. Are there any conflicts between your values and your goals? (e.g., "My value of family conflicts with my goal of working long hours to build my business.")

5. How can you reconcile these conflicts and align your goals with your values? (e.g., "I can set boundaries around my work hours to ensure I have time for my family.")

WORKSHEET 3.1

6. How can you use your values to stay motivated and overcome obstacles when working towards your goals? (e.g., "I can remind myself of my values when I feel discouraged or overwhelmed, and use them as a source of inspiration and motivation.")

Now that you have assessed your values and how they relate to your goals, reflect on how you can use this information to set goals that align with your values, and to stay motivated and overcome obstacles when working towards those goals. Remember to stay true to your values, celebrate small wins, and seek support from others when needed.

WORKSHEET 3.2

Personal Goal-Setting Worksheet

Instructions: Use the questions below to guide you through the process of setting personal goals that align with your values and priorities

1. What are your top 5 personal values? (e.g., family, health, integrity, creativity, growth)

   1.

   2.

   3.

2. Why are these values important to you? (e.g., "Family is important to me because they provide love and support, and give me a sense of belonging.")

   1.

   2.

   3.

WORKSHEET 3.2

3. What are your top 3 personal priorities? (e.g., improving health and fitness, pursuing a hobby, spending more time with family)

1.

2.

3.

4. How can you use your values and priorities to set personal goals? (e.g., "I can set a goal to exercise for 30 minutes every day to improve my health and fitness, or to schedule regular family outings to spend more quality time with my loved ones.")

5. What specific actions can you take to achieve these goals? (e.g., "I can join a gym or workout class to stay motivated, or schedule regular date nights with my partner or family outings to ensure we spend time together.")

WORKSHEET 3.2

6. How will you measure progress towards your goals? (e.g., "I will track my exercise progress in a fitness app, or keep a family calendar to ensure we are scheduling regular outings.")

7. How will achieving these goals benefit your personal life? (e.g., "Improved health and fitness will give me more energy and reduce stress, and spending more time with family will strengthen our bonds and create lasting memories.")

Now that you have set personal goals that align with your values and priorities, create an action plan for achieving them. Identify the specific steps you will take to achieve your goals, and the resources and support you will need along the way. Remember to track your progress, celebrate small wins, and adjust your plan as needed to stay on track towards your goal.

CHAPTER 4:
Strategies for Goal Achievement

CHAPTER 4

Introduction

Achieving your goals requires more than just setting them. It requires planning, commitment, and action. Here are some strategies for achieving your personal and professional goals:

1. Stay focused: Stay focused on your goals by regularly reviewing them, breaking them down into smaller, more manageable tasks, and tracking your progress.
2. Stay motivated: Stay motivated by reminding yourself of your values, visualising your success, and celebrating small wins along the way.
3. Take action: Take action by setting deadlines, prioritising tasks, and overcoming procrastination.
4. Seek support: Seek support from friends, family, colleagues, or a mentor or coach. Having a support system can provide motivation, guidance, and accountability.
5. Stay flexible: Stay flexible by adapting to changing circumstances and adjusting your goals or plans as needed.

CHAPTER 4

Example of strategies for achieving a personal goal:

Goal: "I want to run a 5K race within the next six months."

Strategies:
- Stay focused: Review my goal regularly, break it down into smaller tasks (e.g., running intervals, increasing distance), and track my progress using a running app or journal.
- Stay motivated: Visualise myself crossing the finish line, reward myself for reaching milestones, and seek encouragement from friends or a running group.
- Take action: Set a training schedule with specific workouts and rest days, prioritise my workouts in my calendar, and overcome procrastination by scheduling my workouts at a consistent time.
- Seek support: Join a running group or enlist a running buddy for support and accountability.
- Stay flexible: Adjust my training plan as needed based on my progress or any unexpected circumstances (e.g., injury, weather).

By following these strategies and committing to taking action, you can achieve your personal and professional goals and enjoy the satisfaction and sense of accomplishment that come with success. Remember to stay committed, persistent, and flexible, and to seek out feedback and support from colleagues and mentors along the way.

CHAPTER 4.1

Chapter 4.1
Creating a roadmap for achieving goals

Creating a roadmap for achieving your goals is an effective way to stay on track and measure your progress. A roadmap is a visual representation of your goals and the steps you need to take to achieve them.

Here are some steps you can follow to create a roadmap for achieving your personal and professional goals:

1. Identify your goals: Identify your personal or professional goals and prioritise them based on their importance and urgency.
2. Break down your goals: Break down each goal into smaller, more manageable tasks or milestones. This will help you track your progress and stay motivated.
3. Determine the timeline: Determine the timeline for each task or milestone and create a schedule for achieving them. This will help you stay on track and meet your deadlines.
4. Identify resources: Identify the resources you need to achieve your goals, such as financial resources, equipment, or support from others.
5. Develop a support system: Develop a support system that can help you stay accountable and motivated. This might include friends, family, colleagues, or a mentor or coach.
6. Create the roadmap: Create a visual representation of your goals and the steps you need to take to achieve them. This might include a timeline, a flowchart, or a mind map.

Example of creating a roadmap for achieving a personal goal:
Goal: "I want to learn how to play guitar within the next six months."

Tasks:

- Research and select a guitar.
- Find a guitar teacher or online course.
- Purchase necessary equipment (e.g., tuner, picks).

CHAPTER 4.1

- Practise playing chords.
- Learn to play a song.
- Attend an open mic night.

Timeline:
- Week 1: Research and select a guitar.
- Week 2-6: Find a guitar teacher or online course, purchase necessary equipment, and practise playing chords.
- Week 7-12: Learn to play a song and attend an open mic night.

Resources:
- Guitar teacher or online course.
- Guitar and necessary equipment.
- Practice materials (e.g., songbooks, chord charts).

Support System:
- A friend who also wants to learn to play guitar.
- An online community of guitar players.

Roadmap:
- A timeline that outlines the tasks and milestones for achieving the goal.
- A flowchart that shows the steps and resources needed to achieve the goal.

By creating a roadmap for achieving your personal and professional goals, you can stay on track, measure your progress, and achieve your long-term aspirations. Remember to stay flexible and open to adjusting your roadmap as needed, and to seek out feedback and support from colleagues and mentors along the way.

CHAPTER 4.2

Chapter 4.2
Developing a plan for monitoring progress

Developing a plan for monitoring progress is an important step in achieving your personal and professional goals. Monitoring your progress allows you to track your success, identify areas for improvement, and adjust your plan as needed.

Here are some steps you can follow to develop a plan for monitoring your progress:

1. Identify key metrics: Identify the key metrics that will help you measure progress towards your goals. These might include quantitative measures (e.g., number of sales, hours of practice) or qualitative measures (e.g., feedback from colleagues or customers).
2. Set targets: Set targets for each metric, based on your goals and the timeline for achieving them. These targets should be specific, measurable, and achievable.
3. Track your progress: Regularly track your progress towards your targets, using tools like spreadsheets, apps, or journals. This will help you stay on track and identify any areas where you need to improve.
4. Analyse your results: Analyse your results to identify trends, patterns, and areas for improvement. Use this analysis to make adjustments to your plan and strategies.
5. Celebrate success: Celebrate your successes along the way, no matter how small they may be. This will help keep you motivated and energised to continue towards your goals.

Example of developing a plan for monitoring progress:
Goal: "I want to increase my sales by 20% within the next quarter."

Key Metrics:
- Number of leads generated
- Number of sales calls made
- Conversion rate (number of sales / number of leads)

CHAPTER 4.2

Targets:
- Generate at least 50 new leads per week
- Make at least 20 sales calls per week
- Achieve a conversion rate of at least 40%

Tracking:
- Use a spreadsheet or sales tracking app to track leads, calls, and conversions.
- Set up regular check-ins with a mentor or coach to review progress.

Analysis:
- Analyse the conversion rate by week to identify trends or patterns.
- Review feedback from customers to identify areas for improvement in the sales process.
- Adjust the plan as needed to improve performance.

Celebration:
- Celebrate each milestone reached, such as achieving the target number of leads or calls.
- Celebrate the overall goal achievement when it is met.

By developing a plan for monitoring progress towards your personal and professional goals, you can stay on track, identify areas for improvement, and adjust your strategies as needed to achieve success. Remember to regularly track your progress, celebrate your successes, and seek out feedback and support from colleagues and mentors along the way.

Chapter 4.3
Staying motivated and overcoming obstacles

Staying motivated and overcoming obstacles is a critical part of achieving your personal and professional goals.

Here are some strategies you can use to stay motivated and overcome obstacles:

1. Focus on your why: Stay connected to your why by reminding yourself of your values, your long-term aspirations, and the impact achieving your goals will have on your life.
2. Visualise success: Visualise yourself achieving your goals and experiencing the positive outcomes. This can help keep you motivated and energised.
3. Celebrate small wins: Celebrate small milestones and achievements along the way. This can help you stay motivated and make progress towards your larger goals.
4. Break down barriers: Identify potential obstacles or barriers and develop strategies to overcome them. This might include seeking support from others, developing new skills, or adjusting your plan.
5. Develop resilience: Build resilience by learning from failure and setbacks, and developing a positive mindset that focuses on growth and learning.

Example of staying motivated and overcoming obstacles:
Goal: "I want to run a marathon within the next year."

Obstacles:
- A busy work schedule that makes it hard to find time to train.
- A previous injury that might reoccur during training.

CHAPTER 4.3

Strategies:

- Focus on my why: Connect with my values and long-term aspirations, and remind myself of the positive impact achieving my goal will have on my life.
- Visualise success: Visualise myself crossing the finish line and feeling proud and accomplished.
- Celebrate small wins: Celebrate milestones like running a longer distance or completing a challenging workout.
- Break down barriers: Make a schedule and prioritise workouts, find a running buddy for accountability, and seek professional advice on preventing and treating injuries.
- Develop resilience: Learn from setbacks or injuries, and stay positive and focused on progress rather than perfection.

By using these strategies to stay motivated and overcome obstacles, you can achieve your personal and professional goals and enjoy the sense of accomplishment that comes with success. Remember to stay flexible, persistent, and committed to your goals, and seek out feedback and support from colleagues and mentors along the way.

Chapter 4.4
Celebrating successes and learning from failures

> Celebrating successes and learning from failures are two sides of the same coin when it comes to achieving your personal and professional goals. Celebrating successes can help you stay motivated and energised, while learning from failures can help you make adjustments and improve your strategies.

Here are some tips for celebrating successes and learning from failures:

1. Celebrate small wins: Celebrate each milestone and achievement, no matter how small it may be. This can help you stay motivated and make progress towards your larger goals.
2. Reflect on successes: Take time to reflect on your successes and what made them possible. This can help you identify your strengths and build on them in the future.
3. Share your successes: Share your successes with others, such as friends, family, or colleagues. This can help you build support and momentum towards achieving your goals.
4. Learn from failures: Analyse your failures and setbacks to identify what went wrong and how you can improve. Use this information to adjust your strategies and make progress towards your goals.
5. Reframe failures: Reframe failures as opportunities for growth and learning. Focus on what you can learn from the experience and how you can apply that knowledge to future efforts.

Example of celebrating successes and learning from failures:
Goal: "I want to publish a book within the next year."

CHAPTER 4.4

Successes:
- Completing the manuscript.
- Finding an agent who is interested in representing the book.
- Receiving positive feedback from beta readers.

Celebrations:
- Celebrate each milestone with a special treat or activity, such as going out for a nice meal or taking a day trip.
- Share the successes with friends and family on social media or in person.

Failures:
- Receiving rejection letters from publishers.
- Struggling with writer's block during the editing process.

Learning:
- Analyse the rejection letters to identify common themes or issues, and make adjustments to the manuscript or query letter.
- Seek feedback from colleagues or a writing group to overcome writer's block and improve the manuscript.
- Reframe the failures as opportunities for growth and learning, and focus on making progress towards the goal.

By celebrating successes and learning from failures, you can stay motivated and improve your strategies for achieving your personal and professional goals. Remember to stay positive, persistent, and open to feedback and support from colleagues and mentors along the way.

WORKSHEET 4.1

Career Development Assessment Worksheet

Instructions: Use the questions below to assess your career aspirations and development needs.

1. What are your top 3 career aspirations? (e.g., earning a promotion, developing new skills, starting a business)

    1.

    2.

    3.

2. Why are these aspirations important to you? (e.g., "Earning a promotion will give me more responsibility and financial stability, and developing new skills will keep me competitive in the job market.")

    1.

    2.

    3.

WORKSHEET 4.1

3. What are your current strengths and weaknesses in your career? (e.g., "I am skilled in project management and communication, but could improve my leadership and public speaking skills.")

4. What specific skills or knowledge do you need to achieve your career aspirations? (e.g., "To earn a promotion, I need to develop leadership and strategic thinking skills, or to start a business, I need to learn about business planning and finance.")

5. What opportunities are available to you to develop these skills or knowledge? (e.g., "I can take a leadership course or join a mentorship program to develop my leadership skills, or attend workshops or seminars to learn about business planning and finance.")

WORKSHEET 4.1

6. How can you use your strengths and opportunities to achieve your career aspirations? (e.g., "I can leverage my project management skills and seek opportunities to lead cross-functional teams to develop my leadership skills.")

Now that you have assessed your career aspirations and development needs, reflect on how you can use this information to set career goals and develop a career development plan. Identify the specific steps you will take to achieve your goals, and the resources and support you will need along the way. Remember to track your progress, celebrate small wins, and adjust your plan as needed to stay on track towards your goal.

WORKSHEET 4.2

Professional Goal-Setting Worksheet

Instructions: Use the questions below to guide you through the process of setting professional goals that align with your career aspirations and development needs.

1. What are your top 3 career aspirations? (e.g., earning a promotion, developing new skills, starting a business)

   1.

   2.

   3.

2. Why are these aspirations important to you? (e.g., "Earning a promotion will give me more responsibility and financial stability, and developing new skills will keep me competitive in the job market.")

   1.

   2.

   3.

WORKSHEET 4.2

3. What are your current strengths and weaknesses in your career? (e.g., "I am skilled in project management and communication, but could improve my leadership and public speaking skills.")

4. What specific professional goals can you set to address your development needs and achieve your career aspirations? (e.g., "I can set a goal to attend a leadership course to develop my leadership skills, or to deliver a presentation at a conference to improve my public speaking skills.")

5. How will you measure progress towards your goals? (e.g., "I will track my leadership development through feedback from my mentor or manager, or evaluate my public speaking skills by soliciting feedback from my colleagues or attendees at the conference.")

WORKSHEET 4.2

6. What resources and support do you need to achieve your professional goals? (e.g., "I may need funding or time off from work to attend a leadership course, or practice sessions with a mentor or colleague to improve my public speaking skills.")

Now that you have set professional goals that align with your career aspirations and development needs, create an action plan for achieving them. Identify the specific steps you will take to achieve your goals, and the resources and support you will need along the way. Remember to track your progress, celebrate small wins, and adjust your plan as needed to stay on track towards your goal. Good luck!

CONCLUSION

KEY TAKEAWAYS

Recap of key takeaways

By completing this mini-course and workbook, you have gained the knowledge and skills necessary to set and achieve your personal and professional goals.

In this course, you have learned a lot about goal setting for personal and professional success. Here's a recap of some of the key takeaways:

1. Goals provide direction and focus, and help you achieve your personal and professional aspirations.
2. Effective goal setting requires clarity, specificity, and adherence to the SMART criteria.
3. Personal and professional goals differ in their focus and timeframe, but both require careful planning and commitment.
4. Strategies for achieving your goals include developing a roadmap, monitoring progress, staying focused, staying motivated, taking action, seeking support, and staying flexible.
5. Personal goals should align with your values and priorities, and professional goals should align with your career aspirations and development needs.
6. Overcoming obstacles and setbacks requires resilience, a focus on growth and learning, and a positive mindset.
7. Celebrating successes and learning from failures are critical components of achieving your personal and professional goals.

ACTION STEPS

Action steps for applying goal-setting strategies to personal and professional life

Now that you have learned about goal setting for personal and professional success, it's time to apply these strategies to your own life. Here are some action steps you can take to apply goal-setting strategies to your personal and professional goals:

1. Identify your personal and professional goals: Make a list of your personal and professional aspirations, and prioritise them based on their importance and urgency.
2. Use the SMART criteria: For each goal, use the SMART criteria to ensure that it is specific, measurable, achievable, relevant, and time-bound.
3. Develop a roadmap: Create a roadmap that outlines the steps and resources needed to achieve each goal, including a timeline and milestones.
4. Monitor progress: Regularly track your progress towards your goals, using metrics and targets to measure success and identify areas for improvement.
5. Celebrate successes: Celebrate each milestone and achievement, no matter how small it may be, and share your successes with others.
6. Learn from failures: Analyse your failures and setbacks to identify what went wrong and how you can improve. Use this information to adjust your strategies and make progress towards your goals.
7. Stay motivated: Stay connected to your why, visualise success, celebrate small wins, break down barriers, and build resilience to stay motivated and overcome obstacles.
8. Seek support: Seek feedback and support from colleagues, mentors, or coaches to help you stay accountable and make progress towards your goals.

By taking these action steps, you can apply goal-setting strategies to your personal and professional goals and achieve success in all areas of your life. Remember to stay committed, flexible, and open to feedback and support from others, and to celebrate your successes along the way.

WORKSHEET C.1

Action Planning Worksheet

Instructions: Use the questions below to create a step-by-step plan for achieving your goals.

1. What is your goal? (e.g., earning a promotion, starting a business, improving health and fitness)

2. What specific actions do you need to take to achieve this goal? (e.g., "I need to develop my leadership and strategic thinking skills, or to start a business, I need to learn about business planning and finance.")

3. How long will it take to achieve this goal? (e.g., "I want to earn a promotion within the next 12 months, or start a business within the next 2 years.")

4. What are the milestones or checkpoints along the way? (e.g., "I will complete a leadership course within the next 3 months, or draft a business plan within the next 6 months.")

WORKSHEET C.1

5. What resources or support do you need to achieve these milestones? (e.g., "I may need funding or time off from work to attend a leadership course, or practice sessions with a mentor or colleague to improve my public speaking skills.")

6. How will you measure progress towards your goal and milestones? (e.g., "I will track my leadership development through feedback from my mentor or manager, or evaluate my public speaking skills by soliciting feedback from my colleagues or attendees at the conference.")

7. What potential obstacles or challenges may arise, and how can you overcome them? (e.g., "I may face resistance or competition from other candidates for the promotion, or encounter unexpected expenses or setbacks when starting a business. To overcome these obstacles, I will seek support from my network, seek advice from experienced professionals, or adjust my plan as needed.")

WORKSHEET C.1

Now that you have created a step-by-step plan for achieving your goal, implement the plan and track your progress towards your milestones. Remember to celebrate small wins, seek support from others when needed, and adjust your plan as needed to stay on track towards your goal.

WORKSHEET C.2

Progress Monitoring Worksheet

Instructions: Use the questions below to track your progress towards your goals and make adjustments as needed.

1. What is your goal? (e.g., earning a promotion, starting a business, improving health and fitness)

2. What specific actions have you taken to achieve this goal? (e.g., "I completed a leadership course, drafted a business plan, or started a regular exercise routine.")

3. What progress have you made towards your goal? (e.g., "I received positive feedback from my manager on my leadership skills, secured funding for my business, or lost 5 pounds.")

WORKSHEET C.2

4. What challenges or obstacles have you encountered, and how have you addressed them? (e.g., "I struggled to find time for exercise due to work demands, or faced unexpected expenses when starting my business. To address these challenges, I adjusted my schedule or sought funding from alternative sources.")

5. What adjustments or changes do you need to make to stay on track towards your goal? (e.g., "I need to adjust my exercise routine to make it more manageable, or seek advice from a financial expert to manage expenses more effectively.")

WORKSHEET C.2

6. How will you track your progress towards your goal and make adjustments as needed? (e.g., "I will track my exercise progress in a fitness app, or review my business plan regularly to ensure I am on track towards my financial goals.")

7. What support or resources do you need to achieve your goal and stay on track? (e.g., "I may need a workout buddy or trainer to keep me accountable for my exercise routine, or seek mentorship or advice from experienced professionals to guide my business development.")

Now that you have tracked your progress towards your goal, reflect on your achievements and areas for improvement. Identify the specific adjustments or changes you need to make to stay on track towards your goal, and the support or resources you need to achieve them. Remember to celebrate small wins, seek support from others when needed, and adjust your plan as needed to stay on track towards your goal.

PLANNER PAGES

PLANNING PAGES

These can also be downloaded as PDFs by going to
https://kerrywilliams.uk/gspps

MONTHLY CALENDAR

Month:

MONTHLY FOCUS

Monday	Tuesday	Wednesday	Thursday	Friday	Saturday	Sunday

Goal One
- ☐
- ☐
- ☐
- ☐
- ☐
- ☐
- ☐
- ☐

Monthly Notes

Goal Two
- ☐
- ☐
- ☐
- ☐
- ☐
- ☐
- ☐
- ☐

WEEKLY PLANNER

Monday

Tuesday

Wednesday

Thursday

Friday

The Weekend

NOTES

DAILY PLANNER

Date:

Today's Goal

Tasks
- ☐
- ☐
- ☐
- ☐
- ☐
- ☐
- ☐
- ☐
- ☐
- ☐
- ☐
- ☐
- ☐
- ☐
- ☐
- ☐
- ☐
- ☐
- ☐
- ☐
- ☐
- ☐
- ☐

Appointments
9 am	
10 am	
11 am	
12 pm	
1 pm	

Inspiring Words

NOTES

RESOURCES

Resources for further learning and support.

Congratulations on completing the "Goal Setting for Personal and Professional Success" course! If you want to continue learning and growing in this area, here are some resources you can use:

1. Books: There are many great books on goal setting and personal development, including "The 7 Habits of Highly Effective People" by Stephen Covey, "Atomic Habits" by James Clear, and "Goals!: How to Get Everything You Want Faster Than You Ever Thought Possible" by Brian Tracy.
2. Online courses: There are many online courses on goal setting and personal development, including those offered by Coursera, Udemy, and LinkedIn Learning.
3. Coaching and mentoring: Consider seeking out a coach or mentor who can provide guidance and support as you work towards your goals.
4. Professional organisations: Joining a professional organisation related to your career or industry can provide networking opportunities and resources for career development.
5. Apps and tools: There are many apps and tools that can help you track your progress and stay motivated, including habit tracking apps like Habitica, goal-setting apps like Strides, and mindfulness apps like Headspace.

Remember, achieving your goals is a journey that requires ongoing learning, growth, and support. By using these resources and continuing to develop your skills and strategies, you can achieve success in all areas of your life. Good luck on your journey!

THANK YOU!

Thank You for Completing "Goal Setting for Personal and Professional Success"

Congratulations on completing the "Goal Setting for Personal and Professional Success" mini-course! I hope that the content and exercises provided in this course have been valuable in helping you gain clarity and focus in your personal and professional life.

By completing this course, you have learned the importance of goal setting, the basics of goal setting, and strategies for achieving your goals. You have also gained an understanding of the different types of goals and how to set effective goals using the SMART criteria.

I hope that you have gained practical insights and tools that you can use in your daily life to set and achieve your goals. Remember that goal setting is an ongoing process, and it takes time and effort to achieve your desired outcomes.

I encourage you to continue using the worksheets and exercises provided in this course to further develop your goal-setting skills and achieve your personal and professional aspirations. Don't forget to celebrate your successes along the way and learn from your failures to keep moving forward.

Thank you for choosing this course, and I wish you all the best in your goal-setting journey!

Love Kerry
♥ 😁

FOLLOW ME ON INSTA & FACEBOOK
@IAMKERRYWILLIAMS

HTTPS://KERRYWILLIAMS.UK

Printed in Great Britain
by Amazon